"Lord, teach us to pray."

LUKE 11:1

PRESENTED TO

____

BY

____

ON

____

Teach Me to Pray

Praying God's Word from A to Z

Kristen Wetherell

CROSSWAY®
WHEATON, ILLINOIS

Teach Me to Pray: Praying God's Word from A to Z

Published by Crossway
1300 Crescent Street
Wheaton, Illinois 60187

Cover design, cover and interior artwork: Crystal Courtney

First printing 2025

Printed in China

Hardcover ISBN: 978-1-4335-9909-5

Library of Congress Cataloging-in-Publication Data

Names: Wetherell, Kristen, author.
Title: Teach me to pray : praying God's word from A to Z / Kristen Wetherell.
Description: Wheaton, Illinois : Crossway, [2025] | Audience: Ages 8–12
Identifiers: LCCN 2024045079 | ISBN 9781433599095 (hardback)
Subjects: LCSH: Prayer—Juvenile literature. | Prayers—Juvenile literature.
Classification: LCC BV212 .W474 2025 | DDC 248.3/2—dc23/eng/20250416
LC record available at https://lccn.loc.gov/2024045079

Crossway is a publishing ministry of Good News Publishers.

RRD 34 33 32 31 30 29 28 27 26 25
15 14 13 12 11 10 9 8 7 6 5 4 3 2 1

CONTENTS

INTRODUCTION

WHEN I WAS GROWING UP, my parents had an entire shelf of *The World Book Encyclopedia* in our home office. These were hardcover, glossy books labeled from A to Z—a treasure trove of knowledge! And I loved referencing them. If I had a question, all I had to do was find the subject and read about it. These books taught me so many amazing truths about creation and history. They are now on our family bookshelf, and my kids love learning from them.

Teach Me to Pray is like an "encyclopedia" for prayer. From A to Z, you will find topics, emotions, and situations that are worth praying about—like fear, friendship, mistakes, obedience, worry, loneliness, and many more. All of these prayers are based on God's word, the Bible, which tells us the truth and changes us. You can use the rhyming prayers in this book to talk to God (and you can challenge yourself to memorize the first two lines of each!).

My prayer is that you will open God's word and draw near to Jesus, our Lord and Savior. And, just as my parents passed down their encyclopedias to me, perhaps someday you will give *Teach Me to Pray* to your kids.

Enjoy praying God's word from A to Z!

Kristen

A NOTE TO GROWN-UPS

THANKS FOR CHOOSING *Teach Me to Pray* as a resource for your family and church. Jesus's disciples once said to him, "Lord, teach us to pray" (Luke 11:1). Prayer isn't always easy, which is why we need God's word to help us—yes, even as adults! We can use the words and truths God has given us in his word as we pray and as we teach our kids how to pray. And we can trust his promises: When we pray, God listens. He cares. And, in his timing and according to his will, he responds.

I hope this book serves you and your kids well. While older kids might read this on their own, I encourage you to read it alongside the children you care for, talking about each topic and reading the Bible verses together.

You might use this book:

- as a morning devotional
- at the kitchen table during meals
- during family worship
- before bedtime
- alongside your homeschool curriculum
- in your Sunday school classrooms
- sporadically, as situations arise and the Spirit leads

I count it a great privilege that this book is in your homes and churches, and I am praying the Holy Spirit uses it to equip you as you shepherd the kids God has entrusted to you.

TEACH ME TO PRAY ABOUT

Anger

O God, I'm so angry! I feel so upset!
You're slow to be angry. Don't let me forget!

You're patient with me, and you're gentle and kind.
Your mercy surrounds me before and behind.
In light of your tenderness, help me to see
How slowness to anger can also mark me.
Lord, help me to listen, and then help me speak.
To use self-control doesn't mean that I'm weak.
I thank you that Christ bore your wrath in my place.
My anger's forgiven, for I've received grace.

In Jesus's name I pray, amen.

READ ABOUT IT

"Be angry and do not sin; do not let the sun go down on your anger, and give no opportunity to the devil. . . . Be kind to one another, tenderhearted, forgiving one another, as God in Christ forgave you."

EPHESIANS 4:26–27, 32

THINK ABOUT IT

Have you ever been so angry you could explode? Maybe things didn't go your way, or someone really upset you. There's a good and right kind of anger—a godly, acceptable response toward sin. But there's also a sinful and wrong kind of anger that hurts others with our words and actions. How can we know the difference? We look at who God is: "Slow to anger, and abounding in steadfast love" (Ex. 34:6). God sees all our sin. And rather than giving us what we deserve, he gives us his Son. Every day, God remains patient and gentle with us, giving us a chance to turn away from our sin and turn toward Jesus. So, when we are angry, we can cry out for his help. When our anger leads to sin, we can ask for forgiveness. And when someone sins against us, we can forgive.

LEARN ABOUT IT

Numbers 14:18
Psalm 103:8
James 1:19–20

DO SOMETHING ABOUT IT

Have you been sinfully angry toward someone lately? Confess your anger to God, ask for his forgiveness and help, and then apologize to the person you hurt.

TEACH ME TO PRAY ABOUT

Attitude

Dear God, I need a brand-new start!
Create in me a humble heart.

My heart's a prideful, selfish place.
Would you please fill me with your grace?
I want a mind like Jesus, please,
Who, serving all the least of these,
Became like me so I can be
Filled up with true humility.
Renew my attitude today
So I can bless those in my way.

In Jesus's name I pray, amen.

READ ABOUT IT

"Do nothing from selfish ambition or conceit, but in humility count others more significant than yourselves. . . . Have this mind [attitude] among yourselves, which is yours in Christ Jesus, who, though he was in the form of God, did not count equality with God a thing to be grasped, but emptied himself, by taking the form of a servant, being born in the likeness of men." | **PHILIPPIANS 2:3, 5–7**

THINK ABOUT IT

It's hard to have a good attitude all the time, isn't it? Some days, it feels like we wake up on the wrong side of the bed, and everyone had better stay out of our way! We usually have a bad attitude because we want to do things our own way. But complaining and arguing lead only to unhappiness in our circumstances and relationships. Instead, God wants us to have the attitude of Christ—a humble-heartedness that trusts God's plan for our days and thinks of others before ourselves. It's not easy—but *it is possible* because of Jesus. He humbled himself to serve us in his death and resurrection. And he continues to humbly serve us right now. Why? So we can share in his attitude, take interest in others, and bring him honor and glory in all we do.

LEARN ABOUT IT

Jeremiah 17:9
Psalm 139:23–24
Romans 12:1–2

DO SOMETHING ABOUT IT

If you're struggling with a bad attitude right now, give yourself this challenge: Say nothing negative or critical. Instead, say only what is necessary, kind, and true.

TEACH ME TO PRAY ABOUT

Blessing

O God of all mercies, the God I embrace,
I know I'll be blessed as I trust in your grace.

Please help me remember where true blessing lives:
In Jesus, your Son, and the life that he gives.
I'm sorry for looking for comfort and ease
In things that can't give them, but only displease.
I thank you for giving me many good things
Like family and friends with the blessings they bring.
Your blessings, O God, are eternally true.
They go on forever. I'm thankful for you.

In Jesus's name I pray, amen.

READ ABOUT IT

"O Lord of hosts,
  blessed is the one who trusts in you!" | **PSALM 84:12**

THINK ABOUT IT

What does it mean to be "blessed"? Does it mean God gives us everything we want—good grades, cool clothes, funny friends, and an easy life? Actually, God's blessings are way better than these. They're better than we could even ask or imagine! He wants so much more for us than we want for ourselves. To be blessed is to be completely happy in Christ. According to the Bible, you are blessed (1) when you know your need for Jesus, (2) when your sins are forgiven, (3) when you're adopted into God's family, (4) when his Holy Spirit dwells in you, (5) when heaven is your eternal home—the list goes on and on! True blessing isn't about us getting what we want. It's about God giving us what we need most: a deeper, stronger relationship with him. It's about God's good and perfect plans unfolding in our hearts. It's about trusting him and loving him, now and forever.

LEARN ABOUT IT

Psalm 1
Proverbs 3:13–18
Ephesians 1:3–14

DO SOMETHING ABOUT IT

How long a list of blessings (spiritual or material) can you make? Go ahead and try! (You might use the "Learn About It" verses to help you make your list.)

TEACH ME TO PRAY ABOUT

Boldness

Lord Jesus, I'm praying for loved ones today,
For boldness to tell them that you are the way,

That you are the truth and that life's in your hands.
You overcame death! You crushed Satan's plans!
O Lord, let me speak the right words I should say.
You promise your Spirit will help me obey
And tell my lost neighbors there's hope to be found
In Jesus, our Savior. Please help me abound
With gentleness, love, and respect as I do.
The only one worthy of fear, Lord, is you.

In Jesus's name I pray, amen.

READ ABOUT IT

"Have no fear of them, nor be troubled, but in your hearts honor Christ the Lord as holy, always being prepared to make a defense to anyone who asks you for a reason for the hope that is in you; yet do it with gentleness and respect." | 1 PETER 3:14–15

THINK ABOUT IT

Do you know someone who doesn't yet believe in Jesus? The Son of God once told his disciples that he is the only way to heaven—the only way to enter into the Father's presence (John 14:6). That means there is only *one way* to be rescued from our sin. And we want our loved ones to know this good news! But telling others about Jesus isn't always easy. Sometimes we feel afraid of how people will respond or what they will think of us. Even the apostle Paul (a pastor and preacher) knew he needed boldness (see Eph. 6:19). We need God to fill us with confidence in him so we are ready to tell others about Christ. We can also ask God to prepare us by giving us the right words to say, as well as a heart of gentleness and respect as we say them.

LEARN ABOUT IT

Jeremiah 1:4–9
Matthew 28:18–20
Romans 10:14–15

DO SOMETHING ABOUT IT

Pray for unbelievers by name. You can make a list of the people you love who don't know Jesus. Then pray for one or two of them each night before bed.

TEACH ME TO PRAY ABOUT

Church

Lord, you cherish your church, and you've made us for you!
Please help me to love it the way that you do.

You call us your people, your body, your bride.
For us, you are holy. For our sake, you died.
I pray for my pastor, who cares for your sheep.
Protect him and lead him. Please carefully keep
Your people committed to loving your word—
We long to be faithful to what we have heard.
Lord, strengthen your body to love as you do,
So, shining like lights, we will glorify you.

In Jesus's name I pray, amen.

READ ABOUT IT

"They devoted themselves to the apostles' teaching and the fellowship, to the breaking of bread and the prayers." | **ACTS 2:42**

THINK ABOUT IT

How would you describe "church"? Maybe you love going to church every week, or maybe it's a struggle. Maybe you've never been to church before. God's church isn't just a building. The Bible calls God's church "the body of Christ" (1 Cor. 12:27). Why? The church isn't only a place; it's made up of God's many different people who work together to show the world who Jesus is. God's church is devoted to proclaiming the life, death, and resurrection of Jesus. It serves like Jesus. It teaches the Bible in his name, and it prays for more people to become part of his body. What an amazing gift to be members of God's church and to worship him together! You can praise God for your local church and ask him to protect, guide, strengthen, and mature his people. It is also a gift to our churches and their pastors and ministry workers when we pray for them.

LEARN ABOUT IT

1 Corinthians 12:12–20
Ephesians 4:15–16
Colossians 3:16–17

DO SOMETHING ABOUT IT

Spend some time praying for the leaders of your church. You could ask your parents to help you make a list of names, and then pray through that list.

TEACH ME TO PRAY ABOUT

Confession

I'm sorry, God, for all my sin.
Forgive me, cleanse me from within!

The darkness makes me want to hide,
To hold my secrets deep inside.
Please give me strength to speak what's true,
Confessing all my sins to you!
I praise you that you've covered me
With Jesus's blood that sets me free.
I'll walk in goodness, truth, and light.
In Christ, I'm holy in your sight.

In Jesus's name I pray, amen.

READ ABOUT IT

"If we walk in the light, as [God] is in the light, we have fellowship with one another, and the blood of Jesus his Son cleanses us from all sin. . . . If we confess our sins, he is faithful and just to forgive us our sins and to cleanse us from all unrighteousness." | 1 JOHN 1:7, 9

THINK ABOUT IT

Imagine you're in a dark room. You can't see anything, so you keep stubbing your toes and walking into walls—*ouch*! You don't know how to escape or find anyone to help you. Sounds painful and lonely, doesn't it? When we disobey God and try to hide our sin, we're like people stumbling around in the dark, hurting ourselves and others. The Bible says we even grieve God's heart when we sin (see Eph. 4:30). But there is hope! Christ died to free us from the darkness. Instead of running away from God when we sin, we can run straight to him. We can confess our sins because God knows everything anyway. He wants us to walk in the light of his forgiveness, freedom, and peace. When we tell God everything and say we're sorry, he promises to forgive us and help us.

LEARN ABOUT IT

2 Samuel 12:13
Psalm 51:1–2
John 12:46

DO SOMETHING ABOUT IT

Is there anything that you've been hiding from God or others (like your parents, grandparents, teachers, or friends)? Don't stay in the darkness. Use today's prayer to tell God you're sorry, and then tell others too.

TEACH ME TO PRAY ABOUT

Decisions

Decisions and choices—they make me feel stressed!
Lord, grant me your wisdom to choose what is best.

To make wise decisions is no easy task,
But, God, you give wisdom to all those who ask.
Please teach me your paths, Lord, and show me your ways
To please you and honor you all of my days.
I praise you for people who help me to know
The wisest way forward, the way I should go.
Please soften my heart so I'm wise to obey,
To make right decisions and walk in your way.

In Jesus's name I pray, amen.

READ ABOUT IT

"Where there is no guidance, a people falls,
but in an abundance of counselors there is safety." | **PROVERBS 11:14**

THINK ABOUT IT

Kids make around three thousand choices every day.* Whew! You make decisions about simple things like what to wear and what to eat. You also make hard decisions about what's right and wrong. Decision-making requires wisdom—knowing the best path forward—and some choices require more wisdom than others. When we don't know what choice to make, we can start by asking Jesus. He promises to counsel us through his Holy Spirit as we read the Bible. We can also talk to wise people we trust, like our parents, teachers, pastors, and trustworthy friends. Without guidance, we risk making foolish decisions. But with good counsel, God will lead us in the right and best paths. We don't need to be afraid of decisions, because God uses all of them—even the not-so-good ones—to bring about his perfect plans for his people.

LEARN ABOUT IT

Job 28:28
Psalm 25:8–9
James 1:5

DO SOMETHING ABOUT IT

What decision is on your mind right now? Who could you talk to about it after you bring it to God in prayer? Go to that wise person and ask for help.

*Kaethe Weingarten, "Decision Fatigue, and Tips on Making Consequential Decisions," Migrant Clinician, September 15, 2022, www.https://www.migrantclinician.org/.

TEACH ME TO PRAY ABOUT

Discouragement

O Father God, my heart feels sad.
Please show me Christ and make me glad!

And make my faith and hope so sure
That I will know I am secure.
God, hear my cry. I turn to you!
Please show me all the good you do.
My rock, you're strong and you are near.
I need to know that you are here.
I feel discouraged, down, and sad,
But you're my hope. You make me glad.

In Jesus's name I pray, amen.

READ ABOUT IT

"Why are you cast down, O my soul,
  and why are you in turmoil within me?
Hope in God; for I shall again praise him,
  my salvation and my God." | **PSALM 42:5–6**

THINK ABOUT IT

A disagreement with a parent or friend. A sports competition you lost. A bad habit you can't seem to break. Sometimes life can be discouraging, can't it? Ever since sin entered the world, humans have felt sad, confused, and low. Discouragement is brought on by our own choices, by other people, and by our circumstances. So, what can we do when we feel discouraged? We have a choice: We can either stay "cast down," or we can look up to God. We can give in to complaining, worrying, and sad thoughts. Or we can turn our thoughts to him. This is what Scripture calls *hoping in God*. First, we look away from what is discouraging us. Then we remember Jesus and his perfect love: how he cares for us, protects us, and is always with us. Discouragement will flee as we run to God and choose to worship him.

LEARN ABOUT IT

Joshua 1:9
Isaiah 40:28–31
Philippians 4:8

DO SOMETHING ABOUT IT

When you're discouraged, it can help to write down what's bothering you. Journal some honest thoughts. Then bring each discouraging thought to God in prayer.

TEACH ME TO PRAY ABOUT

Enemies

I pray for all my enemies. Lord, loving them is tough!
Please change my heart and help me trust: Your strength will be enough.

I ask, Lord, that you change their hearts.
Please humble them to know
That friendship is the better, wiser way for us to go.
O Father, please forgive them, for they don't know what they do.
In hurting me, they do not see they're also hurting you.
Please grant me self-control so what I do and what I say
Reflects the heart of Jesus Christ—his love, his peace, his way.

In Jesus's name I pray, amen.

READ ABOUT IT

"Love your enemies and pray for those who persecute you, so that you may be sons of your Father who is in heaven." | MATTHEW 5:44–45

THINK ABOUT IT

Have you ever met someone who treated you badly, made you mad, and seemed to enjoy it? The Bible calls these people our enemies, those who put others down and hurt them. Our natural reaction is to retaliate—to get back at the person who hurt us. But Jesus calls us to something different: loving our enemies. Instead of retaliating, we pray for them. We ask God to change their hearts. We ask for wisdom to know how to respond. And we ask for patience to trust God with the situation. When Jesus was arrested, tortured, and crucified by his enemies, he trusted his Father and he prayed for them. Because Jesus died to make his enemies into friends, he is able to do this for us too. We only need to ask.

LEARN ABOUT IT

1 Samuel 26:11–12, 21–25
Romans 12:17–18
1 Peter 2:21–23

DO SOMETHING ABOUT IT

Think about your enemies. Pray for them by name, asking God to change their heart. Then ask God to help you think of one way you might bless them this week.

TEACH ME TO PRAY ABOUT

Envy

Dear Father, I'm struggling with envy and greed.
Please help me to trust that you're all that I need.

You've given me everything good, right, and true.
The best of these gifts? That I get to know you!
It's easy to want what you've given my friends.
My jealousy burns, and my pride never ends.
O Lord, how I need you to strengthen my heart!
My flesh, it grows weak, and my faith falls apart.
My heavenly treasure, you're perfect and true.
There's nothing on earth that I need besides you.

In Jesus's name I pray, amen.

READ ABOUT IT

"Truly God is good to Israel,
to those who are pure in heart.
But as for me, my feet had almost stumbled,
my steps had nearly slipped.
For I was envious of the arrogant
when I saw the prosperity of the wicked." | **PSALM 73:1–3**

THINK ABOUT IT

Did you know that envy is also called "turning green"? I think of envy as a rotten mold that spreads its ickiness and creates other problems. Think about it: When you want what someone else has—say, a cool bike, a close friend, or a fun opportunity—what effect does it have? Envy often leads to greed, unthankfulness, bitterness, and even unkind words and actions. When we stumble into envy, we can confess it to God, remember his goodness to us in Christ, and ask for his help in fighting envy with gratitude. At the end of the day, only Jesus can truly satisfy our deepest desires. He is the good gift we need most of all.

LEARN ABOUT IT

Proverbs 14:30
1 Corinthians 13:4
Galatians 5:26

DO SOMETHING ABOUT IT

Practice fighting envy by being grateful to God for who he is, for all his good gifts, and for other people. You can thank him out loud or write down a list in a journal.

TEACH ME TO PRAY ABOUT

Fear

O Lord, I'm afraid, and I'm trembling with fear.
But you are my strength, and I know you are near.

I'm scared of the darkness, but why should I hide?
Your light is my guide, and you stand by my side.
Because of your bigness, please help me to see
The size of my fears and how small they should be.
I wait for you, Lord! Make me brave! Make me strong!
For you are my help and my light and my song.

In Jesus's name I pray, amen.

READ ABOUT IT

"The LORD is my light and my salvation;
  whom shall I fear?
The LORD is the stronghold of my life;
  of whom shall I be afraid?" | **PSALM 27:1**

THINK ABOUT IT

What are you afraid of? We live in a fallen world that has been broken by sin, so there are many scary things to fear. But God wants you to know that your fears will grow smaller as your view of him grows bigger. When you are afraid, ask God to help you see how awesome he is. He is almighty, faithful, and perfectly loving. The greatest fear you could ever know—eternal punishment from God for your sin—has been dealt with by Jesus. And if Jesus has taken care of your biggest fear, won't he take care of your smaller fears too? As the psalmist says, "The LORD is my light and my salvation; whom shall I fear?" God's salvation is worth praising him for every single day. He is always with you, and he will help you when you are afraid.

LEARN ABOUT IT

Psalm 46
Isaiah 41:8–10
Luke 12:4–7

DO SOMETHING ABOUT IT

After you name your fears to God, tell them to someone else you trust. This might be a parent, a grandparent, a teacher, or a friend. Ask them to pray for you about these fears.

TEACH ME TO PRAY ABOUT

Friendship

You're loving, Jesus, always true.
I long to have a friend like you!

A friend who loves me faithfully,
Who will not turn aside from me,
A friend whom I can listen to,
To laugh with, love, and point to you.
Of course, there's only one who'll be
The best and perfect friend for me.
I want my friends to know you too.
Make me a faithful friend like you.

In Jesus's name I pray, amen.

READ ABOUT IT

"A friend loves at all times,
  and a brother is born for adversity." | **PROVERBS 17:17**

THINK ABOUT IT

Good friends are a gift from God. The best kind of friend will encourage your faith by pointing you to Jesus and will stick with you through tough times. Finding this kind of friend isn't easy. That's why we need to pray and talk to our parents. You can ask God, who created friendship, to give you a special companion who loves him first and who will also love you. You can also ask God to make you that kind of friend to others: a trustworthy, faithful friend who points people to Christ. You can practice loving your friends well by praying for them, being a good listener, and putting their interests above your own. You can also share your possessions with them and introduce them to Jesus if they don't already know him. Walking with your friends through hardship is another way to reflect God's love: He never leaves or forsakes his friends.

LEARN ABOUT IT

1 Samuel 18:1–5
Proverbs 18:24
John 15:12–17

DO SOMETHING ABOUT IT

Pray for your friends by name. Then tell them how you prayed for them!

TEACH ME TO PRAY ABOUT

Good Works

My heavenly Father, you've rescued my soul.
I live for your praise, and your glory's my goal!

You say I'm your masterpiece, wonderfully made,
Created in Christ so your grace is displayed.
Please help me to know the good works I should do
To love people well and bring honor to you.
Lord, grant me desire and strength to obey.
When good works aren't easy, my heart wants to stray.
I praise you for Jesus, whose good works are true,
Who's made me his workmanship, lovely and new.

In Jesus's name I pray, amen.

READ ABOUT IT

"We are his workmanship, created in Christ Jesus for good works, which God prepared beforehand, that we should walk in them."

EPHESIANS 2:10

THINK ABOUT IT

Have you ever been to an art museum? They are full of unique pieces of art like paintings, sculptures, and sketches. These museums display the beautiful work of talented artists who created masterpieces with their hands. Similarly, God calls us his "workmanship," or masterpieces. We are his work of art, and he created us to bring him honor and praise. After Jesus rescues us by grace, our good works tell the wondrous story of our rescue, just like a painting tells a beautiful story. Sometimes good works come easily—like helping a friend or serving your church. Sometimes good works are hard—like obeying your parents or telling the truth. We need God to give us desire and strength to walk in good works that honor him. We can pray for this and ask him to lead us in the good works he wants us to do, for his glory.

LEARN ABOUT IT

Deuteronomy 10:12–13
Matthew 7:12–13
Philippians 2:13

DO SOMETHING ABOUT IT

Is there something good God is asking you to do, even though it might be hard? Choose to walk in obedience anyway, knowing this gives God honor and will bring you joy.

TEACH ME TO PRAY ABOUT

Gossip

Lord, all you speak is good and true.
Please help me say what pleases you.

With words I've blessed you as I've prayed.
With words I've cursed those you have made.
Forgive me for the times I've used
My words to tear down and abuse.
I long to be a gentle voice
Whose words encourage, heal, rejoice.
Lord, by your Spirit, search my heart!
My heart is where my words must start.

In Jesus's name I pray, amen.

READ ABOUT IT

"No human being can tame the tongue. It is a restless evil, full of deadly poison. With it we bless our Lord and Father, and with it we curse people who are made in the likeness of God. . . . A harvest of righteousness is sown in peace by those who make peace."

JAMES 3:8–9, 18

THINK ABOUT IT

Words are powerful. They can encourage or tear down. They can tell the truth or deceive with lies. They can bring healing or hurt. Like toothpaste squeezed out of its tube, once we say something, we can't take it back. Speaking hurtful words behind people's backs is what the Bible calls gossip (or slander). The mouth speaks gossipy words, but the source of gossip is our hearts. This means we need Jesus to change our hearts first. We can ask him to help us love our neighbors as ourselves and to give us self-control with our words. And we can ask him to replace harsh, deceitful gossip with kind, true, and peaceful speech. If you've been hurt by gossip, pray that God would heal your hurting heart and help you respond in love.

LEARN ABOUT IT

Psalm 141:3
Proverbs 16:28
Luke 6:45

DO SOMETHING ABOUT IT

The next time you want to talk about someone else, ask yourself these three questions: Is what I'm about to say (1) true, (2) kind, and (3) necessary? If the answer is no to any of these, it is better not to speak at all.

TEACH ME TO PRAY ABOUT

Healing

O God, Our Restorer, your healing I seek.
Please comfort the hurting and strengthen the weak.

Bring healing and cleansing, both body and soul.
Redeem all this illness to make our hearts whole!
Above earthly healing, our sin needs a cure.
We need your forgiveness—and hearts that are pure!
We need you to heal us. Lord, help us to trust.
For you know our bodies and know we are dust.

In Jesus's name I pray, amen.

READ ABOUT IT

"Beloved, I pray that all may go well with you and that you may be in good health, as it goes well with your soul." | **3 JOHN 1:2**

THINK ABOUT IT

Sickness and injury usually take us by surprise. They change our plans and keep us from doing what we would like to do. Sometimes, illness can last a long time and make a person's life look very different than it was before. Maybe we are the ones who are sick or injured. Or maybe it's our family member, friend, classmate, or neighbor. We can bow before God in prayer, asking that he would bring healing and hope. God is the ultimate healer. Not only can he heal our bodies and bring us back to good health, but he also heals our souls through Jesus Christ. Apart from Jesus, the great physician, our hearts remain sick with sin. Yet Jesus forgives our sins and gives us brand-new, healthy hearts through his Holy Spirit. This is our hope! Even when our bodies are hurting and wasting away, our hearts can be healed and renewed day by day.

LEARN ABOUT IT

Psalm 103:14
Malachi 4:2
2 Corinthians 4:16

DO SOMETHING ABOUT IT

After you pray for those who need healing, write them a get-well card and tell them what you prayed for them. This will bring them great encouragement!

TEACH ME TO PRAY ABOUT

Honesty

Dear Lord, help me to say what's right,
To speak your truth and walk in light.

Teach me to hate deceit and lies
And any sinful compromise.
I'm sorry, Jesus, for my sin,
For when the darkness seems to win.
You're faithful and your truth endures.
Create in me a heart like yours,
An honest heart that loves what's true,
That longs for peace just like you do.

In Jesus's name I pray, amen.

READ ABOUT IT

"These are the things that you shall do: Speak the truth to one another; render in your gates judgments that are true and make for peace; do not devise evil in your hearts against one another, and love no false oath, for all these things I hate, declares the LORD."

ZECHARIAH 8:16–17

THINK ABOUT IT

Have you ever heard the saying "Honesty is the best policy"? This is true because Jesus is the truth. He created us in his image, to reflect who he is. He's a truth-telling, truth-loving God. So it is the "best policy" to be who Jesus created us to be—people who love the truth and speak the truth to one another. But this isn't always easy. Truth can sometimes be hard to say and hear, even though it's right. We can ask God to help us love the truth and flee from all lying and deception. We can also ask him to help us pursue honesty in a way that makes for peace. Through the Holy Spirit's power, we want to be trustworthy because our God is faithful and true.

LEARN ABOUT IT

Proverbs 24:26
Isaiah 45:19
Ephesians 4:25

DO SOMETHING ABOUT IT

Is there anything you need to be honest about right now? Start by telling God. Then, go and tell the person who needs to hear it (maybe your parents, a sibling, a teacher, or a friend).

TEACH ME TO PRAY ABOUT

Identity

Praise God, I'm in Christ! O my Lord, strengthen me
To be who I am, both forgiven and free.

You've saved and redeemed me. In you, I'm made new,
A brand-new creation and changed, through and through.
I'm sorry, Lord Jesus, for when I forget
The work that you've finished to pay all my debt.
In Christ I am holy, adopted, and loved.
I'm sealed with his Spirit from heaven above.
My purpose and joy are not found in this place,
But Christ is my life, to the praise of his grace.

In Jesus's name I pray, amen.

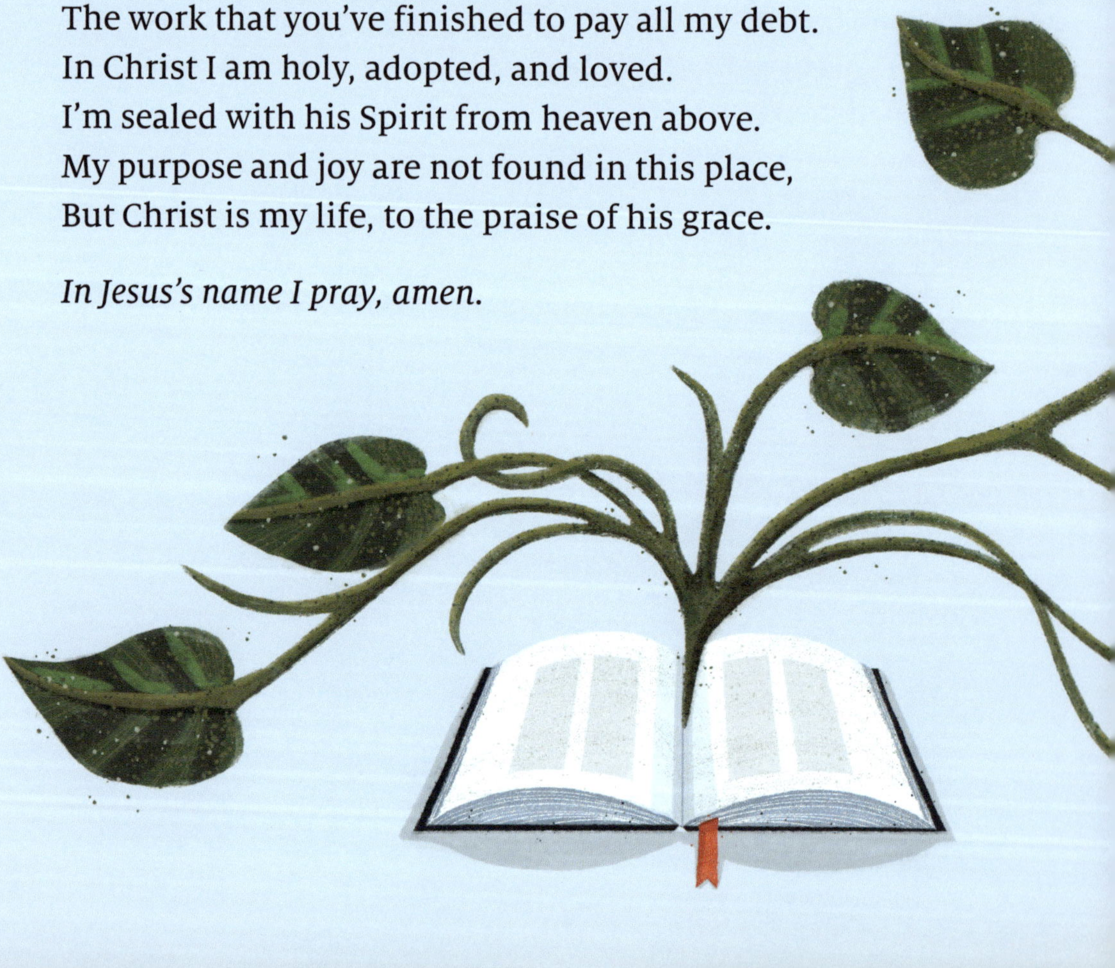

READ ABOUT IT

"If anyone is in Christ, he is a new creation. The old has passed away; behold, the new has come." | 2 CORINTHIANS 5:17

THINK ABOUT IT

What is the most important thing about you? Is it the way you look, or is it what you're good at doing, like playing sports, making friends, or getting good grades? Your answer to this question is usually where you will try to find your happiness. But here's the problem: None of these things can make you happy for very long. Why? Because none of them will last. God tells us in Scripture that the most important thing about us is our identity in Christ. When we trust in Jesus, he becomes our new source of life and happiness—and he never changes! Remembering our true identity isn't easy though. So we need to pray for God's help. We can ask the Holy Spirit to remind us every day of who we are in Jesus and to help us be who we are.

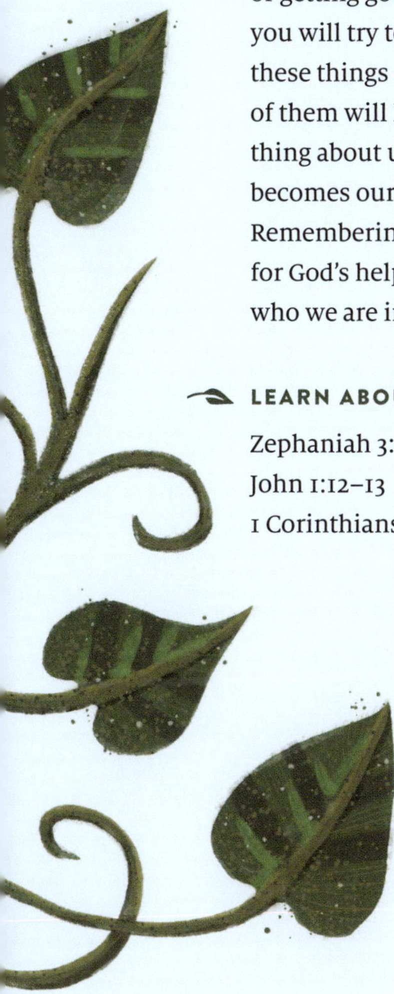

LEARN ABOUT IT

Zephaniah 3:16–17
John 1:12–13
1 Corinthians 1:30

DO SOMETHING ABOUT IT

The whole Bible is God's word and tells us who God is and who we are. The next time you are tempted to place your identity in worldly things, listen to Jesus's voice in Scripture. Then remember that your true identity is found in him.

TEACH ME TO PRAY ABOUT

Influence

O Lord, I long to love what's right,
What's good and perfect in your sight!

Protect my eyes, my ears, my mind
From what would make me dull and blind.
Preserve me so I'm not conformed
To sins around me, but transformed.
I want my heart and life to be
Renewed by what I hear and see.
Then let me be a loving guide
To those you place right by my side.

In Jesus's name I pray, amen.

READ ABOUT IT

"Do not be conformed to this world, but be transformed by the renewal of your mind, that by testing you may discern what is the will of God, what is good and acceptable and perfect." | **ROMANS 12:2**

THINK ABOUT IT

Have your parents or teachers ever told you to "be a good influence" on other people? Influence is your ability to create change. You can be a good influence or a bad one. You can affect people and situations by living for Christ or by living for this world. You can also be influenced by others. Anything (or anyone) you watch, read, or listen to has an effect on you. So we need to be careful about what or whom we allow to influence us. We want our minds and hearts changed for the better because our aim is to worship God and walk in his ways. We can ask God (1) to help us know what influences are good and acceptable; (2) for the wisdom to walk away from those that aren't; and (3) to make us a godly influence on others.

LEARN ABOUT IT

Deuteronomy 4:5–7
Psalm 135:15–18
Matthew 5:29–30

DO SOMETHING ABOUT IT

Make a list of all the "voices" you listen to, including people, shows, podcasts, music, and books. Are these influencing you toward the Lord or away from him? Resolve to set aside anything that would hinder your love for Jesus.

TEACH ME TO PRAY ABOUT

Joy

Dear God, in your presence I want to rejoice,
To lift up my hands and my heart and my voice!

This life isn't easy; it's hard and it's sad.
But you are my joy, and you make my heart glad.
You've given me Jesus, who purchased for me
The joy of forgiveness. He sets my soul free!
In everything help me rejoice as I should,
To trust that you're working all things for my good.
I'll seek you, my joy, and I'll choose to proclaim
That you're my delight. I will praise your great name.

In Jesus's name I pray, amen.

READ ABOUT IT

"You make known to me the path of life;
in your presence there is fullness of joy;
at your right hand are pleasures forevermore." | **PSALM 16:11**

THINK ABOUT IT

In this broken and sad world full of hardship, we are familiar with something called "happiness"—an emotional response to what happens around us. But God's joy is different from happiness. It is based not on our circumstances but in knowing him. This means that even when sad or bad things happen, we can still be joyful, because our God is with us. And he never changes. He is the most joyful being in the universe, and he wants to share his joy with us! He gives us his Spirit of joy who helps us rejoice in everything, especially in Jesus who will never be taken from us. But choosing to rejoice isn't always easy. We need to ask God to fill us with his joy as we look to him, even on the saddest of days. We can ask him to be our highest joy.

LEARN ABOUT IT

1 Chronicles 16:8–10
Isaiah 25:9
1 Thessalonians 5:16–18

DO SOMETHING ABOUT IT

Worship songs that are based on Scripture help us rejoice in the Lord and all he has done. Ask your parents to help you find and play some worship music that will lead your heart to rejoice.

TEACH ME TO PRAY ABOUT

Justice

My righteous God, you always do what's just.
You're never wrong; in you, Lord, help me trust.

But things around me don't seem right or fair.
Injustice reigns and makes life hard to bear.
You say that you're the Judge of all mankind.
Yet in your grace, you heal the deaf and blind!
Because of Christ who bore sins on the tree,
Your justice, Lord, is satisfied for me.
So let your kingdom come and will be done.
Make all things new and righteous through your Son!

In Jesus's name I pray, amen.

READ ABOUT IT

"Shall not the Judge of all the earth do what is just?" | **GENESIS 18:25**

THINK ABOUT IT

"That's not fair!" God has given every person an innate sense of right and wrong. It's not hard for us to know that stealing, bullying, and lying are bad. However, our sense of right and wrong has been twisted by sin. We do not always judge matters rightly. But our God is just, which means that he always does what is right and never does what is wrong. The most unfair thing in the universe is that a perfectly innocent man would take the place of guilty sinners. Yet this is exactly what Jesus willingly did for us on the cross. God's just judgment fell on his Son so that his mercy and grace could fall upon us! We can praise God for not giving us what we deserve and ask him for daily mercies. We can also pray for what's right to abound in our fallen world.

LEARN ABOUT IT

Deuteronomy 32:4
Psalm 67:4
Romans 3:23–26

DO SOMETHING ABOUT IT

Is there someone (or something) you could stand up for? Is there a person or an important cause you can specifically pray for? You might ask your parents, grandparents, teachers, or pastors for some ideas. Then pray together.

TEACH ME TO PRAY ABOUT

Kindness

Your kindness, Father, knows no end!
Your grace I cannot comprehend.

Your goodness came to me in Christ
Through all he gave and sacrificed.
Forgive me, Lord, that I'm inclined
To serve myself and not be kind.
Give me a heart, show me the way
To care for those in need today.
Through all I do and words I say,
Lord, put your kindness on display.

In Jesus's name I pray, amen.

READ ABOUT IT

"When the goodness and loving kindness of God our Savior appeared, he saved us, not because of works done by us in righteousness, but according to his own mercy." | TITUS 3:4–5

THINK ABOUT IT

What is kindness? Kindness is the desire to bless and serve others. It means putting others first, helping those in need, and giving without expecting anything in return. Our motivation for kindness toward others is God's kindness toward us. But kindness isn't easy, is it? Our hearts naturally want to be first and to be served by others. When Jesus came to earth, God's kindness appeared to us in human form. He gave self-centered people like us what we do not deserve. He gave forgiveness, eternal life, and a relationship with himself. He wanted to bless and serve us for our benefit. How might we show kindness to others in response to God's kindness to us? We can ask him to help us reflect his kind heart to others—especially when it's hard.

LEARN ABOUT IT

Micah 6:8
Romans 2:4
Colossians 3:12–14

DO SOMETHING ABOUT IT

What acts of kindness might you do this week? You could pray for someone, welcome a friend at school who is alone, help your parents around the house, or speak kind words.

TEACH ME TO PRAY ABOUT

Knowledge

Lord Jesus, to know you and know your great worth
Is better than anything else on this earth!

It's better than straight A's in science or art—
For knowledge of you always starts in the heart.
Unless I have love, I grow foolishly proud
And become like a noisy gong—clanging and loud.
Please grow me and use me, my knowledge and skill,
To bless those around me and follow your will.
I pray that all knowledge that's good, right, and true
Will reveal your great beauty so people see you.

In Jesus's name I pray, amen.

READ ABOUT IT

"If I speak in the tongues of men and of angels, but have not love, I am a noisy gong or a clanging cymbal. And if I have prophetic powers, and understand all mysteries and all knowledge, and if I have all faith, so as to remove mountains, but have not love, I am nothing."

1 CORINTHIANS 13:1–2

THINK ABOUT IT

Did you know that planet earth is about ninety-three million miles away from the sun? Or that it would take 176 years to drive there in a car? There is so much to know! One of the ways God grows and matures us is through knowledge, our mind's ability to remember information and grasp why it's important. One of the reasons we study in school is to gain knowledge, apply it, and grow in skill. God created our brains for knowledge—but he doesn't want us to stop there. All knowledge has a bigger purpose: to love and honor him. You could be one of the smartest people in the world. Yet if you don't use your intelligence to love God and neighbor, it is useless. We can pray that God will help us grow in knowledge and then use that knowledge for good, to know Jesus more and do his will in the world.

LEARN ABOUT IT

Exodus 35:31
Proverbs 23:12
Ephesians 3:18–19

DO SOMETHING ABOUT IT

Read a story or biography about a Christian who used his or her gifts, knowledge, and love to serve Jesus and his people around the world.

TEACH ME TO PRAY ABOUT

Laziness

Dear Lord, help me serve you in all that I do,
To stop being lazy and work hard for you!

I'm sorry for when I've been idle and dull,
When slothful and lazy, my heart's in a lull.
Instead, make me useful and willing to be
A servant who works for you diligently.
The soul of the sluggard gains nothing at all.
Please help me to listen so I'll hear your call:
"Well done, faithful servant. Receive your reward
And enter my presence, your Savior and Lord."

In Jesus's name I pray, amen.

READ ABOUT IT

"Go to the ant, O sluggard;
consider her ways, and be wise." | **PROVERBS 6:6**

THINK ABOUT IT

Sluggard is a funny-sounding word—but its meaning isn't funny at all. A sluggard is a lazy person, someone who avoids hard work and responsibility. We don't want to be sluggards! Instead, God's word tells us to be like ants. What do ants do? Even though ants are some of the tiniest of God's creatures, they are hard workers with great physical strength. An ant can carry ten to fifty times its body weight! (That's like a human carrying a cow!) Ants work hard to collect, carry, and store food. God wants us to put off laziness and, like an ant, be responsible with what he's given to us. Why? Because, ultimately, we are serving the Lord Jesus Christ. This means we work hard at relationships, school, chores, and other kinds of work. When we pray, we can ask God to forgive us for any laziness and to help us faithfully fulfill all our responsibilities.

LEARN ABOUT IT

Proverbs 13:4
Matthew 25:14–30
Colossians 3:23–24

DO SOMETHING ABOUT IT

Go outside and find an ant colony. Watch the ants at work. Take a few moments to observe the ants, to "consider [their] ways, and be wise."

TEACH ME TO PRAY ABOUT

Loneliness

O Holy Spirit, you are here!
Please help me trust that you are near.

You said that you would come to stay,
So fill me now and every day.
The world's so big while I'm so small.
But you are with me through it all.
And even when I'm on my own
I know I never walk alone.
Lord, be my comfort and my friend.
You're with me always to the end.

In Jesus's name I pray, amen.

READ ABOUT IT

"If anyone loves me, he will keep my word, and my Father will love him, and we will come to him and make our home with him."

JOHN 14:23

THINK ABOUT IT

No one likes to be lonely. You can be in a crowd, surrounded by people, and still feel alone. Sometimes friendships change or people are unfaithful, and we wonder who we can depend on. The Bible gives us our answer: Jesus wants to be with us! God's salvation story includes Jesus's healing of our loneliness by bringing us back to God. God dwelled with us as a human in his Son, and he dwells within his people through his Spirit. Eternal fellowship with God is for all those who receive his Son, and that's a promise! Knowing this, we do not need to despair when we feel lonely. We can cry out to God to remind us of his nearness and love. We can praise him for being our friend who sticks closer than a brother (Prov. 18:24). We can also ask God for dear friends and family members who will walk closely with us.

LEARN ABOUT IT

Joshua 1:9
Psalm 139:7–10
Proverbs 18:24

DO SOMETHING ABOUT IT

Sometimes, when you're feeling lonely, it is good and wise to take the first step toward someone. Who might you be a friend to this week?

TEACH ME TO PRAY ABOUT

Missions

Lord, save the nations! Bring good news,
That all the earth may worship you.

May people bow and tongues confess
Your lordship and your righteousness!
You say we need more feet and hands
To bring your truth, your way, your plans.
Lord Jesus, guide those you will send
So they will go and gladly spend
Their lives to love and follow you!
Please build your church and make her new.

In Jesus's name I pray, amen.

READ ABOUT IT

"How beautiful upon the mountains
are the feet of him who brings good news. . . .
The LORD has bared his holy arm
before the eyes of all the nations,
and all the ends of the earth shall see
the salvation of our God." | **ISAIAH 52:7, 10**

THINK ABOUT IT

Have you ever traveled to a foreign country where people speak another language? It is amazing how many different nations, cultures, and languages are in our world! Even more amazing is that God promises to rescue and gather his people from every nation, tribe, and tongue (Rev. 7:9). How does he do this? He sends missionaries. Missionaries are people who desire to proclaim the good news about Jesus to a dark and lost world. When God's people gather in heaven, we will praise him together. That includes every person who has trusted in Jesus from every nation and language. So we need to pray that God will send more missionaries to do his work! We can also ask God to help us bring his message of salvation to people around us right now.

LEARN ABOUT IT

Psalm 22:27
Acts 1:8
Revelation 7:9–10

DO SOMETHING ABOUT IT

Ask your parents or pastor to help you find a list of missionaries you can pray for. Ask God to strengthen them, make disciples through their ministries, and provide for all their needs.

TEACH ME TO PRAY ABOUT

Mistakes

Lord, my steps and my way are established by you.
I'm tempted to fall; hold me up when I do!

I'm sorry for thinking my own way is right.
I want to obey you with all of my might.
Please grow me in wisdom, and give me your mind,
And help me to love what is true, right, and kind.
You wondrously act for my good and your name
And promise your people will not be ashamed.
Use every mistake to accomplish your plans.
Bring goodness from evil by your perfect hands.

In Jesus's name I pray, amen.

READ ABOUT IT

"The steps of a man are established by the LORD,
when he delights in his way;
though he fall, he shall not be cast headlong,
for the LORD upholds his hand." | **PSALM 37:23–24**

THINK ABOUT IT

Have you ever made a silly mistake? We call people by the wrong name, lose our homework, and sometimes forget to do what our parents ask us to. There are silly mistakes like these . . . and there are serious mistakes. Serious mistakes are foolish and sinful choices that hurt ourselves and others. These are choices we wish we hadn't made. Even though we can't change the past, we can trust God with the future. He can take something bad and turn it into something good, just as he did for his Son. Jesus was killed by hateful men—a most serious and sinful mistake on their part. Yet God used it for our forgiveness and salvation. We can pray that God will help us love his way and walk in his wisdom, and that he will use all our mistakes—both silly and serious—for his good purposes.

LEARN ABOUT IT

Joel 2:24–27
John 18:15–18; 21:15–17
Romans 8:28–30, 37–38

DO SOMETHING ABOUT IT

Can you think of a time when God turned something bad into something good? Think about what you learned through that experience. Consider journaling about it.

TEACH ME TO PRAY ABOUT

Needs

Dear God, all I need, you have promised to give.
Please richly provide all I'm needing to live.

And teach me to bring you my worries and cares,
To trust that you love me and hear all my prayers.
Forgive me for when I confuse what I need
With things that I want. Please help me to plead
According to Scripture and trusting what's best.
Please change my desires and help me to rest.
I'll look at the birds, how they live worry-free,
And know how my Father cares much more for me.

In Jesus's name I pray, amen.

READ ABOUT IT

"My God will supply every need of yours according to his riches in glory in Christ Jesus." | **PHILIPPIANS 4:19**

THINK ABOUT IT

Jesus once taught a lesson about birds. Birds are not anxious, and they do not worry about having what they need. Why not? Every single day their Creator gives them all they need—food, shelter, water, nests, and more. Jesus told his disciples to be more like birds! We often confuse needs with wants. We think that something we desire will make us happy . . . but it won't, at least not for long. God may not give us what we want. Yet he always gives us what we most need. The proof of this is Jesus who satisfies our deepest need: rescue from sin and death. If God gave us his Son, will he not give us everything else we truly need (Rom. 8:32)? We can bring our desires to God in prayer, ask according to his will, and trust him to answer in the best and wisest way.

LEARN ABOUT IT

Psalm 23:1–3
Matthew 6:11, 25–34
Romans 8:32

DO SOMETHING ABOUT IT

Is there a need you can provide for someone else? Perhaps you could pray for someone who is sick, make an offering to your church, or serve an elderly neighbor who can't do housework.

TEACH ME TO PRAY ABOUT

Nervousness

I'm nervous, Lord! My heart beats fast!
Please grant me courage that will last—

The kind of courage Jesus had
When in the garden he felt sad.
He trembled, sweating blood, and cried,
Yet knew that you were by his side.
Please help me know you'll never leave,
And from your strength help me receive
A courage that is strong and true—
Not in myself, but strong in you.

In Jesus's name I pray, amen.

READ ABOUT IT

"Be of good courage, and let us be courageous for our people, and for the cities of our God, and may the LORD do what seems good to him."
2 SAMUEL 10:12

THINK ABOUT IT

When was the last time you felt nervous? Maybe you had to make a speech in front of a room full of people. Or maybe you stood up for someone who was being bullied. It's normal to feel nervous in times like these. Sometimes, doing the right thing or doing a hard thing can make our stomachs drop! We need God to strengthen us and give us courage. We need his help to choose faithfulness, even if the outcome isn't what we would like or expect. Many people in the Bible needed courage against nervousness and depended on God to provide it. Perhaps the greatest example is Jesus. The Son of God was deeply troubled when he prayed in the garden of Gethsemane before his death. So he told his cares to his Father. Jesus trusted the Father's perfect will and found strength to obey. We can do the same.

LEARN ABOUT IT

Deuteronomy 31:6
Isaiah 40:27–31
Luke 22:39–46

DO SOMETHING ABOUT IT

Little acts of courage prepare us for bigger ones. The next opportunity you have to step out in courage, do it! And watch the Lord prepare you for what is next.

TEACH ME TO PRAY ABOUT

Obedience

God, change my heart so I'll obey.
Transform me so I'll love your way!

Your word is good, and it is best.
The Bible stands above the rest.
Within my heart I feel a fight,
Resistance to the way that's right!
Please give me strength to follow you,
To love what's lovely like you do.
Bear forth in me your Spirit's fruit
So holiness is my pursuit.

In Jesus's name I pray, amen.

READ ABOUT IT

"This is the love of God, that we keep his commandments. And his commandments are not burdensome." | **1 JOHN 5:3**

THINK ABOUT IT

When you hear the word *obey*, what do you think about? If we're honest, obedience can seem boring. But what if obedience isn't an obstacle but an opportunity for joy? Our holy God gives us his commands for our good. He invites us into his way, which is always what we need most. This doesn't mean obedience will always be easy or lead to positive outcomes. Jesus's obedience to his Father led him straight to death. But what was on the other side of it? Life! When we say no to our own way and yes to God's ways, we prove our love for him. We also experience true joy—the blessing of staying close to God and walking in his ways. When we pray, we can confess our wrong desires and disobedient choices. And we can ask his Holy Spirit for a heart that loves to obey.

LEARN ABOUT IT

1 Samuel 15:22
Philippians 2:5–11
1 Peter 1:15–16

DO SOMETHING ABOUT IT

The next time you are tempted to disobey, ask yourself, "Who can give me the strength to obey right now?" Looking to Jesus will help you look away from temptation.

TEACH ME TO PRAY ABOUT

Orphans

Lord God, your heart is merciful toward children on their own.
Please comfort them so they will know that they are not alone.

Provide for everything they need; protect them with
your care.
Reveal your Holy Spirit's love so they will know
you're there.
Please give them faith to trust in Christ and turn their
hearts to you.
Adopting sons and daughters—that's what you delight
to do!
I once was lost, but then you found and saved me at
great cost.
Lord, please reveal what I can do to bless and serve
the lost.

In Jesus's name I pray, amen.

READ ABOUT IT

"Father of the fatherless and protector of widows
is God in his holy habitation." | **PSALM 68:5**

THINK ABOUT IT

Did you know that God has a special heart for orphans? An orphan is a child who has lost his or her parents. Maybe you know someone who has been adopted for this reason. Maybe you've heard about people who help orphans in other countries. Or maybe you know the sadness of losing your own parents. God cares for orphans who are without protection here on earth. He loves them so much that he calls us to pray for them and serve them! He is their ultimate protector, just like he protects all his children. It's good to pray for those who need families, asking that God will meet all their needs. We can also praise God for how he adopts all his children into his family. When we trust in Jesus for our salvation, God becomes our Father and Christ our older brother. Amazing!

LEARN ABOUT IT

Psalm 82:3
Zechariah 7:8–10
James 1:27

DO SOMETHING ABOUT IT

Ask your pastor if your church is caring for orphans through partnerships or prayer. Sometimes all it takes for change is one person taking an interest and doing something!

TEACH ME TO PRAY ABOUT

Parents

Dear Father, help my parents be
The hands and feet of Christ to me.

I want to listen and obey,
To trust my parents know the way,
To love and fear and honor you
By showing honor where it's due.
Please strengthen them and help them know
The best and wisest ways to go.
Lord, let me bless them all their days,
And honor them and give them praise.

In Jesus's name I pray, amen.

READ ABOUT IT

"Children, obey your parents in the Lord, for this is right. 'Honor your father and mother' (this is the first commandment with a promise), 'that it may go well with you and that you may live long in the land.'"

EPHESIANS 6:1–3

THINK ABOUT IT

Good parents are a gift from God. No, moms and dads aren't perfect, and they certainly make mistakes. But through loving and faithful parents, God blesses us with his comfort and care. Sometimes it can be hard to trust and follow our parents. Maybe they have sinned against us, or maybe we just don't understand the decisions they've made. We can ask God to help us forgive them, listen to them, and obey them because this is how he designed things to work. We can ask him for a growing relationship with our parents and for healing when we've hurt one another. We can also ask God to give our parents wisdom and endurance to do their jobs well and serve Jesus Christ in everything they do. Above all, we can look to God as our perfectly loving heavenly Father who will always be there for us.

LEARN ABOUT IT

Proverbs 1:8–9
Romans 12:10
Colossians 3:20–21

DO SOMETHING ABOUT IT

Encouraging words build people up and help them persevere. What encouraging words could you speak or write to your parents today?

TEACH ME TO PRAY ABOUT

Peer Pressure

Dear Jesus, the pressures of friends lay a snare.
Please help me to trust in your love and your care.

Deliver me, Lord, from all folly and sin,
And plant godly fear in my heart, deep within.
Mature me in wisdom. Protect me, I pray,
From those who would tempt me to cast off your way.
Lord, give me a care and concern for my peers
That doesn't evolve into ungodly fears.
I want to take refuge in Jesus alone
Who saves me and keeps me as one of his own.

In Jesus's name I pray, amen.

READ ABOUT IT

"The fear of man lays a snare,
but whoever trusts in the LORD is safe." | **PROVERBS 29:25**

THINK ABOUT IT

If your friend jumped off a cliff, would you jump too? What a silly question! But we can make foolish choices when we listen to our friends and not to God. Our peers can pressure us to do the wrong things. So we need to prepare our hearts. When we give in to foolish or sinful choices because of peer pressure, we are struggling with the "fear of man." This means we care more about what people think than what God says. The fear of man tempts us to disobey God, and it leads to destruction. But when we fear God, caring most about what he says, we will be safe in his path and protection. Jesus trusted his Father when he was under great pressure. And because he is the perfect Savior, he will strengthen and deliver you.

LEARN ABOUT IT

Exodus 34:12
Proverbs 1:10
Matthew 6:13

DO SOMETHING ABOUT IT

Just as your friends can pressure you into disobedience, you can influence them for good! What might it look like to lead your friends in a Christ-honoring way this week?

TEACH ME TO PRAY ABOUT

Quarreling

Dear Father, protect me from quarrelsome ways.
Please help me to honor you all of my days.

It's hard not to argue and easy to fight.
I want what I want, and I think that I'm right!
Your word says that folly resides in our hearts,
But fearing you, Jesus, is where wisdom starts.
Please work by your Spirit whose love will control
My words and my actions, and rule in my soul.
I want to be blameless and shine as a light,
So teach me to love you with all of my might.

In Jesus's name I pray, amen.

READ ABOUT IT

"Be not quick in your spirit to become angry,
for anger lodges in the heart of fools." | ECCLESIASTES 7:9

THINK ABOUT IT

When was the last time you got into an argument or fight? Maybe it was with your parents or a friend. Sometimes, we can't even remember why we argued! Scripture tells us that we quarrel because we want the wrong things. We usually want our own way, and we want to control people. So we are quick to become angry toward others. This can happen especially with the people we love and trust the most. But this is foolish because nothing good was ever solved through arguing. We can plead with God to make us wise and humble so the fruit of our hearts isn't quarreling but love, self-control, and peace. We can ask his Spirit to rule our hearts and direct our desires. The same Spirit who worked in Jesus will work in you.

LEARN ABOUT IT

Proverbs 15:18
Philippians 2:14–16
James 4:1–3

DO SOMETHING ABOUT IT

Imagine a disagreement between two people who are quick to listen and slow to speak. With God's help, pursue this kind of dialogue the next time you're in conflict.

TEACH ME TO PRAY ABOUT

Quitting

Dear God, I want to persevere.
I will not quit. I know you're near!

When life is hard, I'll work and wait.
For I have you! Your strength is great!
Please make me steadfast. Help me stand.
When trials come, please hold my hand.
I'll run my race and fight the fight!
I'll look to you with all my might.
You're with me, right now, to the end.
On you, I lean and I depend.

In Jesus's name I pray, amen.

READ ABOUT IT

"I have fought the good fight, I have finished the race, I have kept the faith." | 2 TIMOTHY 4:7

THINK ABOUT IT

Have you ever felt like giving up? Maybe the school project you're working on seems impossible to finish. Maybe you haven't been winning your soccer games. Or maybe you've lost friends because you love Jesus, and you're wondering if he's worth it. When things get hard, it's easy to quit! But God's word promises great rewards for those who don't give up. Those blessings are not always here on earth. We might not see them until we're with Jesus in heaven. When Jesus suffered and faced death, he didn't give in to temptation. He kept his eyes fixed on his Father and finished his race. Now he offers us his strength to stand firm and not quit! We can call upon him, thanking him for his sacrifice and asking him for his support. We can fix our eyes on our eternal reward and finish our race here on earth. That means doing whatever God gives us to do—whether school or soccer or sharing our faith—and not giving up.

LEARN ABOUT IT

1 Kings 19:1–8
Proverbs 24:10
James 1:12

DO SOMETHING ABOUT IT

The prayers of other people can give us strength and help us not quit. Who could you ask to pray for you? Tell them how you're tempted to give up, and ask them to pray for endurance.

TEACH ME TO PRAY ABOUT

Respect

Lord God, I need your help to see
The beauty of authority.

I'm grateful for my mom and dad
And all the teachers that I've had.
Please humble me to know what's good,
And help me listen as I should,
To honor them in all I do,
To trust that they have come from you.
For every person over me,
I praise you for authority.

In Jesus's name I pray, amen.

READ ABOUT IT

"Let every person be subject to the governing authorities. For there is no authority except from God, and those that exist have been instituted by God." | **ROMANS 13:1**

THINK ABOUT IT

It's hard to learn respect for authority. But it's an incredibly important lesson! Our hearts naturally want to be in charge. So God gives us parents, teachers, police officers, pastors, and other adults to teach us to respect *his* authority—his good and righteous rule over all things. Of course, we always need to say no if someone is telling us to sin, and we can ask God to give us wisdom in those situations. But we want our attitudes, words, and actions to be respectful and obedient, even toward imperfect authorities. Jesus is our perfect Savior, and he will strengthen us to be respectful. He not only respected his Father's authority, obeyed his word, and honored his name but he also trusted that evil authorities were ultimately in his Father's hands. Thank God for the leaders he has placed over you, and pray for them to be led by God.

LEARN ABOUT IT

Proverbs 2:1–5
Daniel 1
Ephesians 6:1–4

DO SOMETHING ABOUT IT

Take some time to praise God for the particular authorities he has placed over you. You might write each of them a note to express how important they are to you.

TEACH ME TO PRAY ABOUT

Riches

Lord, help me desire your kingdom and way,
To use what you've given and give it away.

Provide what is good, for you give what I need.
Please help me to put off all envy and greed,
And teach me to treasure the things that you love,
To seek first your kingdom and treasures above.
I'm sorry for when I buy into the lies,
That money and "things" will be what satisfies.
I'm following Jesus; I don't need more stuff!
His heavenly riches are always enough.

In Jesus's name I pray, amen.

READ ABOUT IT

"Provide yourselves with moneybags that do not grow old, with a treasure in the heavens that does not fail, where no thief approaches and no moth destroys. For where your treasure is, there will your heart be also." | **LUKE 12:33–34**

THINK ABOUT IT

Wouldn't it be great if you could buy anything you wanted? You could have the latest gadgets, the coolest clothes, and the most happiness—or could you? Do material things buy happiness? Jesus says they don't. What we want reveals what we love. This doesn't mean we can't earn money or buy things with that money. But it does mean that our money and stuff can't satisfy our deepest desires. Only Jesus can do that. When we ask him to save us from our sinful, wayward hearts, he gives us everything we need. He forgives us, satisfies us, and gives us treasure in heaven. All that is way better than any riches here on earth! We can ask God for new desires and for wisdom to use all our resources well. We can also ask him for a heart that seeks him as our greatest treasure.

LEARN ABOUT IT

Habakkuk 3:17–18
Mark 10:17–31
1 Timothy 6:10

DO SOMETHING ABOUT IT

Do you give a portion of your money to others? You could give an offering to your church, to missionaries, or to a mercy ministry that provides for the poor. There is blessing in generosity.

TEACH ME TO PRAY ABOUT

Scripture

Lord God, your word is pure and true.
Enlarge my heart to hear from you!

Increase my hunger for your voice,
And in your truth, help me rejoice.
Reveal your Son in all I read
So I will recognize my need.
Please use your word to draw me near,
And by your grace, incline my ear.
I want to listen and obey!
Lord, use your word to guard my way.

In Jesus's name I pray, amen.

READ ABOUT IT

"All Scripture is breathed out by God and profitable for teaching, for reproof, for correction, and for training in righteousness, that the man of God may be complete, equipped for every good work."

2 TIMOTHY 3:16–17

THINK ABOUT IT

Is the Bible a book of rules, telling you what to do? Is it a history book that gives you information? Or is the Bible about you? The answer to all these questions is "yes—but . . ." Scripture includes rules, history, and encouragement—but overall it is one big story about how Jesus saves his people. Above everything else, the Bible is how God speaks to us. Why? So we will know him, love him, and look more like him. Many things can keep us from Scripture: distractions, lack of desire, even lies about it ("It's boring!"). But nourishing our souls with God's word is the most important thing we can do. It's how we grow our relationship with Jesus, and it's how we become more like him. We can ask God to give us a hunger for his word as we open our Bibles and listen to his voice.

LEARN ABOUT IT

Psalm 119:9–16
Isaiah 55:10–11
John 6:63

DO SOMETHING ABOUT IT

What is one small change you could make to spend more time with Jesus through Scripture?

TEACH ME TO PRAY ABOUT

Self-Control

Dear Jesus, I'm sinful. Please help me to fight!
Your Spirit's control helps me do what is right.

Your grace has appeared, and you've covered my sin,
And now you've created new longings within.
I long to be holy, to use self-control,
To flee what is evil and safeguard my soul.
Lord, train me in goodness and help me be wise,
Just like a strong athlete who runs for the prize.
The fruit of your Spirit comes only from you,
So help me to love you and do as you do.

In Jesus's name I pray, amen.

READ ABOUT IT

"The fruit of the Spirit is love, joy, peace, patience, kindness, goodness, faithfulness, gentleness, self-control; against such things there is no law." | GALATIANS 5:22–23

THINK ABOUT IT

What is self-control? We often think it's saying no to bad things, like junk food, hurtful words, or bad habits. But what if self-control is also about saying yes? Self-control is the Spirit-empowered ability to say no to sin and yes to God—his will, word, and ways. The world tells us to "follow our hearts," but our hearts are the problem. To bear the fruit of God's Spirit, we need new hearts and new desires. We need self-control. This is what Jesus offers us. He was perfectly self-controlled, saying no to sin and yes to his Father. So he is the perfect Savior, covering us in his goodness as we trust in him. We can cry to Jesus, asking him to help us fight sin and pursue self-control and all its good fruit. He promises to help those who call upon him.

LEARN ABOUT IT

Proverbs 25:28
1 Corinthians 9:25
Titus 2:11–14

DO SOMETHING ABOUT IT

Identify one virtue of the Spirit's fruit that you want to grow in, and ask God to help you pursue it.

TEACH ME TO PRAY ABOUT

Temptation

Dear Father in heaven, temptation is hard.
Please help me to flee it and be on my guard!

My heart is deceitful. My enemy's strong.
But you are my strength, my salvation, my song.
Please always provide an escape I can take
When temptation invites like that slippery snake.
Please help me to see the destruction sin makes,
That sin never gives—only kills, wrecks, and takes.
O Lord, you were tempted and tried, just like me;
And now you're my hope to stand firm and to flee.

In Jesus's name I pray, amen.

READ ABOUT IT

"No temptation has overtaken you that is not common to man. God is faithful, and he will not let you be tempted beyond your ability, but with the temptation he will also provide the way of escape, that you may be able to endure it." | 1 CORINTHIANS 10:13

THINK ABOUT IT

Temptation is like a rodent trap. Something yummy lures a mouse or rat—like a bit of cheese or fruit. And it looks good to the rodent as it approaches. But then, *wham*! That yummy-looking cheese brings sudden disaster. Similarly, temptation looks good, but it ends in destruction. When Adam and Eve gave in to temptation, they wanted something for themselves rather than wanting God's way. They listened to lies instead of listening to God. Temptation will entice us in the same way. But God promises that he will always give us an escape. And that way is usually listening to his word. When Jesus was tempted by Satan, he wielded God's word like a sword, escaped temptation, and defeated his enemy. In his strength, so can we!

LEARN ABOUT IT

Genesis 4:7
Matthew 4:1–11
Ephesians 6:10–18

DO SOMETHING ABOUT IT

What is one thing you are tempted to do right now? Choose a Scripture verse—a command, warning, or promise of God—that you can use to fight against this temptation.

TEACH ME TO PRAY ABOUT

Thankfulness

I thank you, Lord, for you are good!
You give me way more than you should.

I don't deserve your lavish grace,
Your mercies, or your warm embrace.
Please help me see all that you've done
Through Jesus Christ, your perfect Son.
I'll sing to him and speak his praise
Just as I'll do for endless days.
Please fill my heart with thanks to you
For all you are and all you do.

In Jesus's name I pray, amen.

READ ABOUT IT

"Rejoice always, pray without ceasing, give thanks in all circumstances; for this is the will of God in Christ Jesus for you."

1 THESSALONIANS 5:16–18

THINK ABOUT IT

Imagine that you are a royal king or queen, ruling over your kingdom. You give your subjects everything they need: food, shelter, work, land, and freedom. But your subjects never once say thank you. They take what you offer but never recognize your generosity. How would this make you feel? Unfortunately, we can be like these people. We take God's gifts but rarely pause to thank him for his goodness. Sometimes we're also slow to say thank you to others. But God wants us to be full of gratitude! Because he gave us Jesus, we can trust him with everything else he gives us. Where would we be apart from God's generosity? He saves us and provides all we need. We can praise God for his character, works, and gifts—not just sometimes but all the time.

LEARN ABOUT IT

1 Chronicles 16:8–10, 34
Psalm 28:7
Colossians 3:15–16

DO SOMETHING ABOUT IT

Start a thankfulness journal. At the end of each day, write down three things you're thankful to God for. Then use this list to help you praise him.

TEACH ME TO PRAY ABOUT

Unborn

Lord, bless the unborn, all the babies you've made.
Protect them and care for them. Come to their aid!

Deliver them safely, and please make them strong,
And set them apart so to you they'll belong.
Creator and Savior, you give life its start.
We're made in your image. We're formed in your heart.
You knit us together. You planned all our days.
All life's from your Spirit; we live for your praise.

In Jesus's name I pray, amen.

READ ABOUT IT

"Your eyes saw my unformed substance;
in your book were written, every one of them,
the days that were formed for me,
when as yet there was none of them." | **PSALM 139:16**

THINK ABOUT IT

Do you know someone who has a baby? Babies are adorable! All of us once started as babies. And even before that, God had each of us in mind. He planned to create us. Every human being is made in God's image, by his power. We live because he gives us life! The world will tell you that only certain people have worth and value. Yet Scripture tells us that *all* people do, even the tiniest babies in their mothers' wombs. We need to pray for the unborn, that God will preserve their lives, protect them, and grow them strong to follow Jesus. What a privilege we have to pray for those who cannot pray for themselves!

LEARN ABOUT IT

Genesis 1:27; 2:7
Job 33:4
Psalm 139:13–15

DO SOMETHING ABOUT IT

If you know a mother who is pregnant, pray for her child. Then tell her you prayed! It will deeply encourage her heart.

TEACH ME TO PRAY ABOUT

Ungodliness

Lord God, you have placed me right here and right now.
Prepare me to follow you; please show me how!

I want to be changed by your Spirit and power.
I know that I need you to help every hour.
The world will persuade me to follow my heart,
But knowing my heart is the right place to start.
My heart is deceitful, but you, Lord, are true!
So set me apart for allegiance to you.
This world's not my home, but in heaven I'll bow
Before you, King Jesus. Prepare my heart now.

In Jesus's name I pray, amen.

READ ABOUT IT

"Understand this, that in the last days there will come times of difficulty. For people will be lovers of self, lovers of money, proud, arrogant, abusive, disobedient to their parents, ungrateful, unholy . . . having the appearance of godliness, but denying its power. Avoid such people." | 2 TIMOTHY 3:1–2, 5

THINK ABOUT IT

Imagine you're an astronaut going to another planet. When you land on the surface, you notice how different it is from your home planet. You feel like a stranger there! The Bible tells us that God's people are strangers here on earth. This place is not our final destination or forever-home. Because of this, one of our greatest challenges is to live in this world without becoming like it. Ungodliness is the opposite of who God is, and it surrounds us. Apart from God changing our hearts, we naturally love ourselves and want our own way. Some of these pursuits can even seem good! But Jesus trains us to say no to the world and yes to him. We can ask God to help us wait with self-control and godliness for Jesus to bring us home to heaven.

LEARN ABOUT IT

Jeremiah 5:20–23
Titus 2:11–14
James 4:4

DO SOMETHING ABOUT IT

What is one way you let the world influence you toward ungodliness? Confess that to the Lord and ask him to help you walk in godliness instead.

TEACH ME TO PRAY ABOUT

Vanity

Lord, all of life is shifting sand,
So help me value what will stand!

When pride appears and rears its head,
Remind me that I'm dust instead.
The grass, it withers. Flowers fade.
But your great name will be displayed!
Your word continues on and on;
Your kingdom, I can rest upon.
In Jesus, life is not in vain;
Your purpose and your word remain.

In Jesus's name I pray, amen.

READ ABOUT IT

"The grass withers, the flower fades,
but the word of our God will stand forever." | ISAIAH 40:8

THINK ABOUT IT

If you were to make a list of your current skills and abilities, what would you write down? Are you athletic? Artistic? Great at making friends? Maybe you're highly intelligent or musical or you love books. These are all good pursuits, and every good gift comes from God. But someday, all our abilities will fade. The Bible says our lives are like a mist that is here and then gone. Only one thing will last, and that is God's word. The kingdoms of this world will come to an end, but the kingdom of God will endure forever! Anytime we feel prideful about our abilities and struggle with vanity, we can remember how our lives are like a mist. What matters most is our walk with Jesus and the transforming work he is doing within us. Someday, heaven and earth will pass away. So we can ask God now to help us value what's most important.

LEARN ABOUT IT

Psalm 62:8–10
Ecclesiastes 1:14
Mark 13:31

DO SOMETHING ABOUT IT

One way to remember this truth is to read history. Truly, nothing is new under the sun! Grab a biography or history book and remind yourself of how temporary earthly life is.

TEACH ME TO PRAY ABOUT

Vocation

God, make me skilled in what I do,
To use my gifts to honor you.

By grace, I want to persevere
In moving toward a good career,
To serve, obey, and follow you
In any pathway I pursue.
Direct me, guide me how to live,
To use the giftings that you give.
In everything I am and do,
Please help me, Lord, to worship you!

In Jesus's name I pray, amen.

READ ABOUT IT

"Do you see a man skillful in his work?
He will stand before kings;
he will not stand before obscure men." | **PROVERBS 22:29**

THINK ABOUT IT

What do you want to be when you grow up? A doctor? A teacher? A mom or dad? An astronaut, artist, or athlete? It's fun to think about what career God might have us do someday. We can bring all things to the Lord in prayer, including our future work in life. The big word for your life work is *vocation*. The Bible tells us that every skill and ability comes from God, and that he wants us to use those abilities for his honor and praise. You don't have to pursue a "religious" vocation to follow Jesus. You can do *all things* for him—even art, medicine, and teaching! Ask God to help you see what you're good at doing. Then ask him to give you the desire to use those skills to help others.

LEARN ABOUT IT

Genesis 2:15
Exodus 35:30–35
Acts 18:1–4

DO SOMETHING ABOUT IT

Is there a particular vocation you're interested in? Ask someone who works in that vocation if you can shadow him or her for a day and learn about the ins and outs of the job.

TEACH ME TO PRAY ABOUT

Waiting

Come quickly, Lord Jesus. Renew everything!
I long for your presence, my Savior and King.

I wait for the day when you'll come back for me,
To deal with all evil and set your world free.
For now, make me watchful, attentive, awake
To flee from all sin and to live for your sake.
And when I'm unsure what tomorrow will bring,
Please help me believe that you know everything.
I wait for you, Lord. Make me strong as I do!
For you are the one who'll make everything new.

In Jesus's name I pray, amen.

READ ABOUT IT

"Christ, having been offered once to bear the sins of many, will appear a second time, not to deal with sin but to save those who are eagerly waiting for him." | **HEBREWS 9:28**

THINK ABOUT IT

When is it hard for you to wait? In line at the amusement park? Until dessert? To get taller so you can dunk a basketball? Everybody waits for something. Yet only believers in Jesus eagerly wait for him. God's word tells us that he's coming back! Jesus appeared on earth to rescue us, and he will appear once again to return for us. Jesus will take believers to live with him forever. And he will make all things new. We will finally see his face and be free from all sin and hardship. Until Jesus returns, we wait. We can pray for patience and a greater longing to see him. We can also pray that we will love and obey him until he comes. And we can ask him to help us trust him with all the other things we're waiting for here on earth.

LEARN ABOUT IT

Daniel 7:13–14
Isaiah 40:28–31
Luke 12:35–40

DO SOMETHING ABOUT IT

Two ways we can eagerly wait for Jesus are by listening to him (reading the Bible) and talking with him (praying). How might you pursue these two things this week?

TEACH ME TO PRAY ABOUT

Worry

Dear Lord, when worry's at its worst,
I long to seek your kingdom first!

Transform my heart, renew my mind
To think on what is pure and kind.
Increase my trust that you will give
All things I truly need to live.
From sinful worry help me flee
And make me like a planted tree
Whose roots run deep and fruit is sweet,
And does not fear tomorrow's heat.

In Jesus's name I pray, amen.

READ ABOUT IT

"Do not be anxious about your life, what you will eat or what you will drink, nor about your body, what you will put on. Is not life more than food, and the body more than clothing? . . . But seek first the kingdom of God and his righteousness, and all these things will be added to you." | **MATTHEW 6:25, 33**

THINK ABOUT IT

Have you heard anyone say, "Don't be a worrywart"? A "worrywart" is an anxious person, someone who can't stop thinking about the worst possible scenarios. While you may not be a worrywart, all of us worry sometimes. Jesus knows this. That's why he told his disciples not to be anxious about anything. He reminded them that they couldn't add one minute to their lives by worrying. Worry doesn't do anything good for us! If God gave you his only Son, he will also give you everything else you truly need. You can pray that God's Spirit will help you think about what is true and helpful and that his peace will replace your worries. Pray also that God will help you seek him above everything else.

LEARN ABOUT IT

Jeremiah 17:7–8
Luke 10:38–42
Philippians 4:4–8

DO SOMETHING ABOUT IT

The next time you feel worried, tell God exactly what you're worried about. Get specific. Imagine placing your worries and fears into his good and trustworthy hands.

TEACH ME TO PRAY ABOUT

eXcellence

Lord Jesus, I worship your excellent way.
I want to know more of your beauty each day!

Please open my eyes to your fullness and grace,
The glory of God in your beautiful face,
So like your friend Moses I'll shine with your light
And show forth your glory like stars in the night.
Please help me approve what is lovely and true,
To ready myself for the day I meet you.
O Lord, you are excellent, wholly divine.
I'm yours, now and always, and Jesus, you're mine.

In Jesus's name I pray, amen.

READ ABOUT IT

"You are a chosen race, a royal priesthood, a holy nation, a people for his own possession, that you may proclaim the excellencies of him who called you out of darkness into his marvelous light." | **1 PETER 2:9**

THINK ABOUT IT

Who is your favorite superhero? Even the best, strongest, most courageous hero cannot compare to Jesus. He is the most excellent person in the universe. He is altogether lovely, perfectly good, and completely trustworthy. He laid down his life to rescue us from our archenemies: sin, death, and Satan. Jesus is a true hero! When we have him, we have everything. He will never fail us. He will always be faithful to us. He is excellent in every way. And as we worship and follow him, we become more like him. We can proclaim his excellencies to a dark and lost world that desperately needs a hero. Pray that God's Spirit will reveal to you how excellent Jesus is and enable you to tell others of his excellencies. What a privilege!

LEARN ABOUT IT

Psalm 150
Isaiah 25:1
Philippians 1:9–11

DO SOMETHING ABOUT IT

Write in a journal and finish this sentence: "Jesus is excellent because ________." See how many reasons you can give for his excellent greatness!

TEACH ME TO PRAY ABOUT

eXistence

Lord God, you created all things for your fame.
I live for your glory and for your great name!

I thank you, wise God, for your purpose and plan.
You had me in mind before all things began.
I'm sorry for when I forget why I'm here,
To know you and love you and hold Jesus dear,
To honor and praise him with all of my heart!
Please help me remember you've set me apart.
You've chosen and called me to make your name known.
I live for your name! I'm no longer my own.

In Jesus's name I pray, amen.

READ ABOUT IT

"[Jesus] is the image of the invisible God, the firstborn of all creation. For by him all things were created, in heaven and on earth, visible and invisible, whether thrones or dominions or rulers or authorities—all things were created through him and for him." | COLOSSIANS 1:15–16

THINK ABOUT IT

Why are you here? Are you here to become popular, to do amazing things, to change the world? Or do you exist for some other purpose? God's word is clear: You exist for Jesus. He created you to know him and then to show his beautiful glory to the world. God made you for a relationship with him. Everything else you do—other relationships, skills, vocations, accomplishments—is meant to point to Jesus. No matter what happens, nothing can take away Christ's love or change your purpose. You exist to know God and make him known. Ask God to give you a passion for this purpose and a desire to seek Jesus in everything you do.

LEARN ABOUT IT

Ecclesiastes 3:11
Romans 11:36
Revelation 4:11

DO SOMETHING ABOUT IT

Do people you know need to be told about (or reminded of) why they exist? How might you bring this good news of great purpose to them this week?

TEACH ME TO PRAY ABOUT

Yesterday

Dear Jesus, when my sins feel large,
Help me to know that you're in charge!

Your promise stands, and you forgive.
My past is gone; in you I live.
My sins removed more than I'd guessed,
They're farther off than east from west.
Please train my eyes to look to you,
Away from old, and toward the new.
I press on toward the upward call:
I seek you. You're my all in all.

In Jesus's name I pray, amen.

READ ABOUT IT

"One thing I do: forgetting what lies behind and straining forward to what lies ahead, I press on toward the goal for the prize of the upward call of God in Christ Jesus." | PHILIPPIANS 3:13–14

THINK ABOUT IT

Have you ever wished you could change the past? Maybe you said something you regret or did something you wish you hadn't, even just yesterday. God says in his word that dwelling on the past isn't always helpful. Instead, we can learn from it and press forward, leaning into God's mercy and grace found in Jesus Christ. We remember that God calls us to look at his Son, not at ourselves or our history. In him we find forgiveness of sins and hope for change through his Spirit. We find a willing Savior and faithful friend who will not reject us. We can ask Jesus to help us press on in following him in the present as we trust his full forgiveness for the past. And we can also extend this same mercy and grace to others.

LEARN ABOUT IT

Psalm 103:12
Isaiah 43:16–21
Hebrews 12:1–2

DO SOMETHING ABOUT IT

Do you need to extend mercy and grace to someone this week? Brainstorm with a parent, friend, or family member what that might look like.

TEACH ME TO PRAY ABOUT

Youth

Dear Father in heaven, I know I'm so young.
But I'm an example, in conduct and tongue!

In Jesus, you rescue; for sin, you atone.
And then you appoint us to make his name known.
I'm sorry for when I lose sight of your way,
Forgetting my actions are meant to display
Your holiness, purity, kindness, and peace!
Conform me to Christ. May his Spirit increase
And fill and transform me—my soul, mind, and heart!
Lord, make me your vessel and set me apart.

In Jesus's name I pray, amen.

READ ABOUT IT

"Let no one despise you for your youth, but set the believers an example in speech, in conduct, in love, in faith, in purity."

1 TIMOTHY 4:12

THINK ABOUT IT

Who is your favorite person in the Bible? Some of the most encouraging stories of faithfulness come from young people—just like you. You don't have to be a certain age to trust and follow Jesus. And you don't need gray hair to be wise! When God rescues us, he makes us holy and uses us for his purposes. This means that God can use you! Even though you are young, you can be an example for others in the way you speak and act. Your love, faith, and desire for holiness can point people to Jesus, who is the image of God. Ask God to draw you to Christ in faith, and then ask him to make your life count for him!

LEARN ABOUT IT

1 Samuel 3:19–21
2 Kings 22:1–2
Luke 2:52

DO SOMETHING ABOUT IT

Are there young people (either kids or young adults) who have made a difference in your life and pointed you to Jesus? Tell them! It will encourage them to keep pursuing godliness.

TEACH ME TO PRAY ABOUT

Zeal

May love for you, Jesus, consume all of me,
So fill me with zeal to the highest degree,

To treasure you more than all music and sports
And friendships and contests and science reports.
Lord, fill me with passion for you above all,
To live for you, God, in the big and the small.
Like Jesus was zealous for you and your way,
Consume me with longing to know you today.
I want to be fervent in spirit for you!
So teach me to serve you in all that I do.

In Jesus's name I pray, amen.

READ ABOUT IT

"Do not be slothful in zeal, be fervent in spirit, serve the Lord."

ROMANS 12:11

THINK ABOUT IT

Have you ever seen a professional sports game, like football or soccer? It's usually loud and crazy, with fans shouting and waving their arms! Fans show a lot of passion and enthusiasm—what the Bible calls "zeal." What is God zealous for? His own glory and the good of his people. He's zealous for a relationship with you, which is why he sent his Son, Jesus, to rescue sinners. It's fun to be zealous for things we enjoy, like sports, music, and friendships. But above everything, believers in Jesus are called to be zealous in serving him. This is our privilege! So when our zeal for God is weak, or when we're tempted to love other pursuits more than him, we can confess this to him. We can ask Jesus, by his Spirit, to increase our zeal—to make us more passionate about him than anything else in this world.

LEARN ABOUT IT

Psalm 119:137–140
John 2:13–17
Philippians 3:1–11

DO SOMETHING ABOUT IT

Read about Christians who were zealous for Christ. Notice some of the ways they grew in their faith and zeal for God.

TEACH ME TO PRAY ABOUT

Zion

I need you, Lord! I call on you!
Come quickly, and make all things new!

I need you more than words can tell
To rescue me from death and hell.
Lord Jesus, you alone can save
And resurrect me from the grave.
I cannot wait to see your face,
When justice reigns and sin's erased.
Until that day, Lord, keep my soul,
And come and make creation whole.

In Jesus's name I pray, amen.

READ ABOUT IT

"Sing aloud, O daughter of Zion;
shout, O Israel!
Rejoice and exult with all your heart,
O daughter of Jerusalem!
The LORD has taken away the judgments against you;
he has cleared away your enemies.
The King of Israel, the LORD, is in your midst;
you shall never again fear evil." | ZEPHANIAH 3:14–15

THINK ABOUT IT

Can you imagine a world without any evil? There would be no sin, sadness, or suffering. There would be no temptation or pain. Here's the amazing news: This new world is quickly coming. The Bible story tells us how God will restore his people and his world. And that includes us! When we call on the name of the Lord Jesus, admitting our need for him to save us from our sin, he rescues us. He forgives us. He gives us a new heart. Our salvation starts at that moment, and it continues into eternity. Often when the Bible talks about Zion, it is referring to our final home, a new heaven and new earth that we will enjoy forever. And the best part is that Jesus will dwell with us there. We will finally see his face! We can ask God to keep our eyes fixed on Zion. In the meantime, we'll pray for Jesus to return and make all things new. And if you haven't asked Jesus to save you, you can do that—right now.

LEARN ABOUT IT

Psalm 14:7
Joel 2:32; 3:16
Revelation 21:1–4

DO SOMETHING ABOUT IT

Have you seen your desperate need for Jesus to save you from your sin? Why not ask him to do that right now? You can even ask a parent, pastor, or friend to pray with you.